The Story of
CHARLES DICKENS

The Story of

CHARLES DICKENS
The First Celebrity Writer

———————

By Andrew Billen

Previously published as *Who Was... Charles Dickens* in 2005
and as *The Boy Who Invented Christmas* in 2009 by Short Books
Unit 316, ScreenWorks
22 Highbury Grove
London N5 2ER

This hardback edition published as part of the "Great Victorians"
series in 2017 by Short Books

10 9 8 7 6 5 4 3 2 1

A CIP catalogue record for this book is available
from the British Library.

ISBN 978-1-78072-321-1

Cover illustration © Evie Dunne
Cover design by Daniella Shreir

Printed and bound in Great Britain by CPI Group (UK) Ltd,
Croydon, CR0 4YY

For Annie

PROLOGUE
A Carol is Read

Have you ever had a story read to you by someone really good at reading aloud? I don't just mean someone who can hold your attention and doesn't stumble or flick through the pages to see how much further it is to the end of the chapter. I mean someone who can read to a group and make everyone think the story is being told just to them, someone who can do the different voices without sounding daft, someone who actually seems to turn into the characters as they speak. I mean someone who can make you laugh out loud one minute and make you cry the next.

Perhaps you know a reader as good as that. Now imagine someone who was ten times as talented, a person so brilliant that they could charge money to read to hundreds of people at once. And now imagine that this fellow – for it is a man I am thinking of –

also wrote the story, just as he wrote scores of others, all of them so much admired that people agreed he was the greatest writer in the world. The man you are imagining is Charles Dickens and, as we begin his story, he is about to begin reading.

It does not matter much where he was. It could have been the town hall in Birmingham, which is where in the Christmas of 1853, at the age of 41, he began this second career performing his own work. But it could have been in any number of towns and cities where he performed in the next sixteen years, earning a great deal of money for himself: London, Reading, Peterborough, Sheffield, Coventry, Rochester, Edinburgh, Dublin, Belfast, Darlington, Huddersfield, York, Halifax, Scarborough, Brighton, Preston, Bradford (where one time 3,700 people came) or Folkestone. Maybe he is not in a town hall, but in a theatre, a warehouse, a bookseller's, a hotel or even a carpenter's shop (as he was in Folkestone). As for the audience, anyone might be in it, young and old, famous and unknown, poor and rich. One time Queen Victoria came. In Birmingham, where it all began, Dickens insisted that tickets should be sold for just a few pennies so that most people could afford to come.

Wherever he was and whoever he was performing to, the staging would be the same. He would stand behind a low reading desk that was covered with a red cloth. On each side of it were small ledges, on the right for his water, on the left for his gloves and handkerchief. At the bottom of the desk's legs was a rail for resting his foot on. Behind him was a large maroon screen, the same shade as the carpet before him. Against this backcloth, his face would be brightly lit by gas lamps so everyone could see his expressions. In his hand he would hold a copy of the book, its pages marked with notes to himself such as "cheerful" or "stern", but he had rehearsed so carefully he would hardly glance at it. There was one rule he had: no one was allowed to sit behind him. One of his hobbies was hypnotism, and maybe these audiences were half-hypnotised themselves. He wanted everyone to look into his bright, intelligent eyes that half the time crinkled with good humour and half the time were as sorrowful as a spaniel's.

At eight o'clock precisely, he stepped on to the stage. He was not a tall man but he was slim and held himself well. His long brown hair was parted on the left and had a tendency to fly away from his scalp. A moustache almost covered the top of his mouth and then came down the sides to join a raggedy goatee beard that fell so far down his chin that sometimes it hid his bow tie. He would wear a dark suit but a colourful waistcoat, across which stretched the chain of his gold watch. From his buttonhole sprouted a rose or a geranium. Even when he was not on stage, there was something very theatrical about Charles Dickens.

As he walked on stage, he would be met by loud applause. He would pretend not to notice and, only when it had finally died down, would he speak. "My good friends," he'd begin, a slight hissing sound accompanying that final "s". There would be more clapping because everyone felt they knew him so well that he was a friend. And, in a way, they did know him, for books usually tell us something about the people who have written them and Dickens's books do that more than most. His are full of versions of the people he met and knew and mocked and loved and feared. Acquaintances would sometimes write to him protesting about how they had been "used" in his novels. His books also contain many versions of Dickens himself as a boy, a young man, a husband and a father. But on the page these characters take on their own life and become something different again.

Some of the characters have become almost more famous than the books they are in. Even if you had never heard of *The Pickwick Papers*, you would probably recognise Mr Pickwick, that jolly stout figure with a bald head and circular spectacles. If, as I hope you will, you read *Nicholas Nickleby*, you will not forget Nicholas with his scarf and his sweep of dark hair or his silly, over-chatty mother whom Dickens based on his own. But you are even less likely to forget the horrible schoolteacher – Wackford Squeers, with his single eye when "popular prejudice runs in favour of two". You may not have yet read *Oliver Twist* but you probably know the film *Oliver!*. I bet you remember the name of the shrivelled old thief with the "villainous looking and repulsive face" who captures Oliver and trains him to pick a pocket or two: it's Fagin. Dickens was best of all at thinking up creepy characters. Pip is the young hero who tells the story of *Great Expectations* but just as important to the story is Magwitch, the escaped prisoner he meets on the marshes, a fearful limping man "soaked in water, smothered in blood, and lamed by stones". If Magwitch does not make your flesh crawl then Miss Havisham, whom Pip meets not long after, certainly will. Ditched by her fiancé on her wedding day, she lives alone in an old house where she is dressed in her tatty bridal dress and surrounded by the food and decorations prepared for her wedding reception. At the end of the book, her ragged wedding gown catches on fire. Yet her death is not as grisly as that of Krook, the withered old keeper of the rag and bottle warehouse in *Bleak House*: without anyone's help he just explodes, his "glutinous ashes" ending up clinging to the walls and ceiling.

A famous painting shows Dickens snoozing on a chair by his desk while around him float characters from his books. It is splendid, but it does not show a fraction of the people he invented. By one calculation his books contain 3,500 characters, good, bad, rich, poor, young, old, tragic, comic – every one different. The books they were born into are still to be found in every library and decent bookshop today, from *The Old Curiosity Shop* to *A Tale of Two Cities*. They were all good enough in themselves to be immediate bestsellers but there is another reason why people were so excited by them. In those days it was the custom to publish novels chapter by chapter in a magazine, so that a new episode would appear every month. Like a television soap opera today, the stories got people hooked. On publication day people would queue outside bookshops waiting for them to open.

Sometimes the latest chapter would contain terrible news. In the winter of 1840 it seemed as if the whole world was following the story of Little Nell, the thirteen-year-old heroine of *The Old Curiosity Shop* who wanders the country with her grandfather, the owner of the junk shop. Finally she is worn out by exhaustion and the strain of looking after the old man. In New York, Americans gathered at the harbour waiting for the new chapter to arrive by boat. "Is Little Nell dead?" the crowds called out to the British passengers as they disembarked. In England Lord Jeffrey, a famous judge who liked to read Dickens while juries were out considering their verdicts, broke down in tears when he read that she had, indeed, died. An Irish politician tossed the magazine out of the compartment of the train he was on, yelling: "He should not have killed her!"

So when he read to his devoted fans, Dickens well knew how to move them to tears. Luckily, he knew just as well how to make them laugh. But he also knew how to make them think, particularly about people less fortunate than themselves.

There was one story that, above all, he enjoyed reading aloud. It starts with the words: "Marley was dead: to begin with. There is no doubt whatever about that." They are gloomy words but also very well chosen for they introduce the best ghost story ever written, an unusual ghost story with a happy ending but the sort of happy ending that makes you cry and makes you think. The book is *A Christmas Carol*.

CHAPTER ONE
A Happy Start

For the first eight Christmases of Charles's life it snowed. Just as today, Christmas two hundred years ago was a time for families to gather round the fireplaces in their own home, and the snow just made it even cosier. Like all children, Charles loved Christmas and his parents made sure it was extra special. His father, John Dickens, was the son of a housekeeper who worked for a rich family called the Crewes. In Crewe Hall, where he had been brought up, they took Christmas seriously. That is to say they took it very unseriously: with lots of dances, games, charades, conjuring, laughter, turkey and plum pudding. By the time John was a parent, he was determined that in his smaller home he would still take Christmas very seriously.

One of his son's earliest memories was of a New

Year's Day party. He remembered being carried in a woman's arms – perhaps his mother's, perhaps his nurse's – and getting dizzy looking down to the hallway below. Downstairs, ladies and gentlemen were sitting in a long row against a wall, drinking from little glass cups with handles. But he could remember nothing else. He must have been very young.

What he never forgot were the toys he was given. There was a Noah's ark that "was not found seaworthy when put in a washing tub" and whose animal passengers were not to scale (the fly was only a bit smaller than the elephant). There was a donkey whose fur seemed real, a great black horse with red spots all over him, and something called a Jacob's ladder made of little squares of red wood that clattered over one another. Some of his toys scared him. Couldn't the fat tumbling man not just lie down and stop staring his lobster eyes at him? The toy demon who jumped out of a box also leaped out at him in his dreams. Most alarming of all was a paper mask grown-ups put on for fun. Sometimes Charles would wake up sweating and shouting "Oh, I know it's coming! Oh, the mask!" His sister's doll's house seemed to him a much safer toy.

Until he was ten, Charles lived with his family mainly in Kent on the mud flats of south east England. Yet another sort of boy might have been quite unhappy – Charles was a puny, weak youngster, unable to join in the games of marbles and spinning tops with the same enthusiasm as other boys. He suffered often from a severe pain that would run down his left side – a complaint he would have to put up with all through his life and which he blamed on an inflamed kidney. But, for Charles, these years were about as magical as any child's could be. As a boy, he watched the other children play, and got his fun out of observing life from a distance. This is what writers do.

Charles's mother was called Elizabeth, a small, pretty, sparky woman with a good sense of humour and a tongue that sometimes ran away with itself. She had married John when she was 19. He was four years older with a steady job with the Navy pay office. He was a chatty, cheerful man who loved words almost as much as his son would. He liked to dress up ordinary thoughts in fussy language. For example, he would rather say "I must express my tendency to believe his longevity is (to say the least of it) problematical" than "I do not think he will live long".

He was a generous man who could not afford to be as generous as he was. In fact, he had a problem with money: he was always spending more than he had and borrowing more than he could repay. He could not really afford the rent on the pleasant house on the outskirts of Portsmouth in Hampshire where Charles was born on Friday, 7th February 1812, so in the summer John, Elizabeth, Charles and his two-year-old sister, Fanny, moved to a cheaper area. The children didn't care. From their new house they could see the soldiers from the local fort marching by and they were often taken down to the docks to see the sailors landing.

When Charles was just three, his father was posted to work in London. Charles was too young to remember much about the move and, in any case, two years later, they returned to the country. On a hot summer's day, they arrived back in Chatham in Kent where John had a been given a better job in the dockyards. The Dickenses' new house was big. Set behind iron railings, it looked out upon a field full of daisies and buttercups down to the marshes of the River Medway. An old lady lived next door and next door to her was a retired naval officer who smoked cigars in his front garden. On the other side lived a peach-faced little girl called Lucy whom Charles promptly fell in love with.

His first lessons were given by his mother. She taught him the alphabet from a book. "A" stood for an Archer who shot at a frog. "Z" was for Zebra. When he was six he and Fanny were sent to school. He hated it. It was run by an old woman who dressed in black and smelled of musty lavender and kept a snappy pug dog. Since she used to beat her pupils with a birch stick it is perhaps not surprising that Charles did not enjoy his lessons. Still, it is funny to think that Charles, the great writer, did not at first like reading and even formed an "intense disgust" for printers and printing. "As time wore on, however," he wrote, "and I became interested in story-books, this feeling of disgust became somewhat mitigated. I encountered a bean-stalk – that marvellous bean-stalk up which Jack climbed to the Giant's house!"

He may have not at first liked to read but he liked stories! A young servant in the house called Mary would tell him tales about a certain Captain Murderer who killed his wives and baked them into pies, and about a ship's carpenter called Chips who sold his soul to the devil. Soon he was reading on his own. One Christmas Eve he read *Little Red Riding*

Hood and soon he moved on to *Tales from The Arabian Nights* and *Robinson Crusoe*. On summer evenings while the other boys played boisterously in the churchyard he would lie on his bed at the top of the house lost in a book.

Unlike Charles's teacher, John Dickens believed in making life fun for children. He was also very good at telling stories but most of all he liked walking, a love that his son would share. One of their favourite excursions was to the nearby town of Cobham. It took them through shady woods and out on to an open park where deer chomped in front of Cobham Hall. They would have a drink at a pub by the church in Cobham and then make their way home. At Gad's Hill they passed a big red brick house with tall bay windows and a bell tower. Charles liked it so much that one day his father said to him: "If you were to be very persevering, Charles, and were to work hard, you might some day come to live in it."

When Charles was nine, a sixth child, Frederick, was added to the family. Life was getting very expensive for his parents. John, who loved partying and entertaining, was soon suffering from money worries or what he called "some temporary embarrassments of a pecuniary nature". He was an optimist, however, always expecting "something to turn up". Unfortunately, it rarely did and not long after Frederick was born, the family moved to a cramped house in the poorer part of town. There were no more parties, but Charles remained contented. He was now at a much better school run by a young man whom he liked called William Giles and was doing well. Dressed in a blue jacket, broad white collared shirt, waistcoat and tightly buttoned trousers, with a white hat over his curly hair, Charles would walk to school quite happily.

One of his great loves was the theatre. He often visited his local playhouse, the Theatre Royal in Rochester, a "sweet, dingy, shabby little country theatre" that he believed much larger than the theatres in London until, that is, he was actually taken one Boxing Day to a see a pantomime in London. The plays at the Rochester theatre were often "stupid" and "badly acted". When he saw Shakespeare's Richard III, about a wicked hunchback king, he noticed how the night before the big battle Richard slept on a sofa much too short for him. When he saw Shakespeare's Macbeth he noticed that the witches in it looked very similar to the ordinary people of Scotland in later scenes. But did it matter? Not at all. He loved acting and actors and when his aunt's boyfriend later took him behind the scenes at an amateur theatre he found he loved it all even more.

He already knew how to stand up and entertain a room. One poem he would recite to the family was about a lazybones who did not want to get out of bed:

'Tis the voice of the sluggard; I heard him complain,
You have wak'd me too soon, I must slumber again.

His nurse recalled that he accompanied the words "with such action and such attitudes". In a clear treble voice, he sang the pop songs of the day and even some he had made up himself. His father was so proud that in the local bars, he would often lift his son up on to a chair and get him to sing. At the end he would be cheered. Most interestingly, considering how he would later entertain thousands by doing almost the same thing, he would perform "monopolylogues" in which he would play all the parts in a short play.

Everyone thought he was talented, but Charles knew he was special. He had read enough and seen enough to realise that if he worked hard there might be a future ahead of him brighter than working in an office like his father did. Then, suddenly, that childhood of white Christmases and summer walks ended, and with them, or so it seemed, all of Charles's great expectations.

CHAPTER TWO

Lost in London

It was the worst Christmas of his life. It was 1822, Charles was ten, and his father had been transferred to work at Somerset House by the Thames. Before leaving, John, now badly in debt, had sold anything worth anything from the home in Chatham. Now in London, he found the cheapest practical place to rent; a narrow, dingy, terraced house of four rooms, a basement and an attic in Camden Town. In these times this part of north London was a run-down area, half town, half country, whose gloomy meadows, scattered with rubbish tips, were nothing at all like Chatham's hay fields. At the end of the street was a burial ground. In the distance dimly peered the dome of St Paul's.

For a few weeks, Charles remained in Chatham to finish the Christmas term at William Giles's but then he was plonked on a stage coach to join the family in London. "Through all the years that have since passed," he later wrote, "never have I lost the smell of the damp straw in which I was packed – like game – and forwarded, carriage paid, to the Cross Keys, Wood Street, Cheapside, London. There was no other passenger inside, and I consumed my sandwiches in solitude and dreariness, and it rained hard all the way, and I thought life sloppier than I had expected to find it."

The house he arrived at was crowded. Inside were his parents, his five brothers and sisters (including a new baby), the nurse who had replaced Mary (she had married and needed to stay behind) and James Lamert, the stepson of the man his aunt had dated and then married, who was lodging with them while waiting to join the army.

Quite soon his older sister Fanny left. Although it meant more room, Charles was upset for two reasons. First, he would miss her very much. Second, she had gone off to study piano at the Royal Academy of Music on a course that would cost their father almost twice as much as the yearly house rent. It seemed terribly unfair. In Chatham, Charles had been the star, now his sister seemed on the first rung of a career on the stage while he did not even have a school to go to. Charles could not understand it. His father was a kind-hearted man, yet, Charles concluded, he had "utterly lost at this time the idea of educating me at all." Charles had fallen into a state of neglect.

He was not *totally* neglected however. James Lamert built him a small model theatre as a kind of substitute. Held together with paste and glue and gum, it had scenery painted in watercolours before which the "actors", cardboard cut-outs from a pattern book, were moved about on wires. Charles put on two plays: *The Miller and His Men* and *Elizabeth or the Exile of Siberia*. But the toy theatre was not a substitute for education. For a while, he turned to books. "They kept alive my fancy, and my hope of something beyond that place and time." However his father took them to a pawnbroker's shop where they were exchanged for a small sum of money.

With nothing else to do, Charles cleaned his father's boots, helped his mother look after the other children and ran small errands for neighbours. To while away time, he took to wandering around the area, staring into the windows of the shops, cafés and factories. As he got bolder, he strayed further south, walking through Holborn down to the City of London itself. What he saw often alarmed him. He ran across a mad woman dressed all in black but with bright red painted cheeks. Another old lady was rushing off to church in her bride's outfit – as she did every day, a figure he would recall when he came to write about Miss Havisham in *Great Expectations*.

One day, out sightseeing with a grown-up friend of his parents, and with only a few pence in his pocket, he actually managed to get lost. It led to a most extraordinary adventure. When he realised that he had lost sight of the grown-up in a crowd, he was terrified. He asked the way to Guildhall, where the mayor of London held dinners, somehow confusing it with a Gold Hall made of gold. On the way he suddenly felt so tired, he lay on the ground and fell asleep. When he awoke, he was hungry so went into a baker's shop to buy a cooked sausage. He was just eating it when a black dog came up. He shared with him a bit of his sausage, and decided to call him Merrychance. Showing no thanks, Merrychance growled and tore the rest of the sausage out of his hands. Charles burst into tears but soon pulled himself together and set off again, rambling on through the yards and courts and little squares that made up the City, peeping into counting houses and running off when he was spotted. At the Royal Exchange, where merchants traded, he came upon a bunch of shabby men munching biscuits and decided they must have put all their money into a sailing expedition and were now desperately waiting for their boats to come back in. At the Mansion House, the home of the Lord Mayor, he spied on the chefs at work in their white caps. A cook with black whiskers, caught his eye and shouted: "Cut away, you sir!"

"I suffered very much all day, from boys," Charles remembered. "They chased me down turnings, brought me to bay in doorways, and treated me quite savagely, though I am sure I gave them no offence. One boy, who had a stub of black-lead pencil in his pocket wrote his mother's name and address (as he said) on my white hat, outside the crown. MRS BLORES, WOODEN LEG WALK, TOBACCO-STOPPER ROW, WAPPING. And I couldn't rub it out."

But there was one good thing about this frightening day. At the end of it he still had enough money to go to the theatre. He paid his sixpence and sat at the back next to a baker who spent most of the performance kissing his girlfriend. A short comedian with a fat face told jokes and sang songs and then proposed to raffle the donkey he was sitting on. Charles worried he might actually win. Luckily, the man behind him who had been eating smelly fish, won instead. Charles enjoyed the rest of the show very much more.

When he got out of the theatre it was a dark, moonless, wet night and now he really panicked. He ran about shouting "I am lost" until he bumped into a watchman, a kind of policeman employed in those days to guard the streets at night. The watchman was old and feeble and had a terrible cough that forced him to lean against a wall until each fit had passed, but he led Charles to the nearest watch house. Exhausted, the boy fell asleep by the fire. When he awoke it was to see his father's face looking down on him. When Charles later wrote about this day, in an essay called *Gone Astray*, he insisted this was exactly how it had happened: "They used to say I was an odd child, and I suppose I was. I am an odd man perhaps."

This was not Charles's only adventure in his early days in London. He would travel to Limehouse to see his godfather, a prosperous man called John Huffam (John and Huffam were Charles's own middle names) who made ship's rigging. Down here on the Thames, he passed docks and ship breakers yards, old hulks stranded in mud, little oyster boats, creaking wooden piers and rotten wharfs. The river was fearful, "overcast and secret, creeping away so fast between the low flat lines of shore: so heavy with indistinct and awful shapes, both of substance and shadow: so deathlike and mysterious." On his journeys back he would ride in a carriage through the strange glooms and flaring lights of London's crowded streets. "Streams of people apparently without end poured on and on, jostling each other in the crowd and hurrying forward, while vehicles of all shapes and makes, mingled up together in one moving mass like running water…"

It was a fearsome place but he had only seen its surface, not its dark depths. He had not seen the south banks of the Thames by Rotherhithe where the people would lower buckets and pans into the river so as to have something to drink and wash in. He had not visited the slums and gutters where lived the unwashed figures who ran to and fro among the pigs, sheep and oxen at Smithfield Market. He had not seen the alleys where young women were murdered at the dead of night. Nor had he watched a murderer hanged. Not yet.

The centre of London was a maze of narrow streets

far too small for the millions who were pouring into the capital looking for work. In one small area nearly three thousand people would be jammed in fewer than a hundred houses. What sewers existed were usually clogged or broken. Urine and excrement trickled down gutters in the middle of streets and emptied into the Thames from which drinking water would then be piped up into stand pipes on the streets. The city stank of the manure of horses and not just of horses. Fogs often lay over the city – white, green and yellow, made up of the smoke of coal fires, factories and steamboats. Some days it grew so thick that the sunlight was blocked out and people lit torches to see their way even though it was still daytime.

In such conditions disease spread quickly: cholera, typhus, diarrhoea, dysentery, smallpox and fevers. If you were poor you would be lucky to live beyond the age of twenty-two (the average age at death was, in any case, only twenty-seven). The graveyards were not big enough to contain the dead so bodies would be piled on top of one another. And where there was poverty and disease there was also crime: pick-pocketing, mugging, prostitution and murder. The punishment was either years in overcrowded jails or death. Hangings were public affairs. Crowds gathered early

31

for the best view and, afterwards, celebrated with, as Charles would later write, "ribaldry, debauchery, levity [and] drunkenness".

It was into this London, from which he had so far been protected by his father's over-stretched salary, that Charles would now be thrown.

CHAPTER THREE
The Poor Boy

Shortly after Charles's second Christmas in Camden, the family moved nearer to the centre of town. With John Dickens sinking ever deeper into debt, a plan had been devised for his mother to open a school in their new and bigger house. A brass plate with the words "Mrs Dickens's Establishment" was screwed to the front door and Charles and the maid went up and down the streets posting pamphlets advertising the new school through letter boxes. But no pupils ever came. The only visitors to 4 Gower Street North were those to whom his father owed money. They came at all hours and they were angry.

A dirty-faced boot maker turned up at seven one morning. "Come!" he yelled. "You ain't out yet, you know. Pay us will you? Don't hide, you know, that's mean. I wouldn't be mean if I was you. Pay us, will you? You just pay us, d'yer hear!" Inside, John Dickens hid, his face covered with anguish and shame. He grabbed a razor – one of those open knives men used for shaving – and gestured that he was going to cut his throat. Elizabeth screamed and told him to put it down. But once the cobbler had gone, John quickly cheered up and, humming a tune, left for work.

John and Elizabeth knew the truth, however. They had run out of money and needed to earn some urgently. Just at this moment something, as John would say, did turn up, although it was a "something" that dismayed Charles. James Lamert, the kindly man who had built Charles his toy theatre, had recently left the Dickens home and, tired of waiting for the army to take him on, was running a small business for his cousin, a shoe polish factory making bottles of what was called Warren's Blacking. James offered Charles a job at it – not an interesting or well-paid job but no worse, he knew, than many children took. For six shillings a week (about twenty pounds in today's money), he would work twelve-hour days from eight in the morning until eight at night, with an hour off for lunch and half an hour for tea.

His parents were delighted: perhaps the money Charles would earn would save them. But although

James said he would try and give him lessons in the lunch hours, Charles was horrified: he wanted to go to school not to a factory! He could not understand why his parents could not see the unfairness of this happening to a child of such "singular abilities, quick, eager, delicate and soon hurt". He felt the victim of some "dark conspiracy" to thrust him into the world before he was ready.

But it was no use complaining and nor did he, at least not out loud. Two days after his twelfth birthday, he got up early and walked the mile or so to Warren's Blacking at Hungerford stairs, just where Charing Cross railway station is now. His first impression of the factory was of dirt, decay and rot. Grey rats rattled around the cellars and squeaked and scuttled up the stairs to where everyone worked. At first Charles was seated away from the other boys in an alcove in the counting house. His job was to cover the tops of the pots of polish with paper and paste labels on their sides. As he worked, he looked through a grimy window out at the Thames, watching the coal barges that passed downstream past his uncle's business in Limehouse and on down to Kent and the happy places of his childhood.

After a few days he was moved into the general

workroom. Here he was introduced to some rough boys, unlike any he had met before. One was Paul Green, whose father was a fireman at Drury Lane Theatre. Another lad wore a paper cap and a tattered apron and was called Bob Fagin (a name, you recall, Charles would use in *Oliver Twist*). They were not bad boys and Bob in particular was kind, but Charles did not find it easy to mix with them. They called him the "young gentleman", which only made Charles feel more out of place.

Within two weeks of taking up this job an even greater calamity befell the family. A baker had complained he was owed a great deal of money and John was arrested for debt. He was taken first to a halfway house where debtors were given a last chance to pay up before they were sent to jail. But, pursued by other creditors, some even from his Kent days, and unable to persuade his relatives to help, on 20th February 1824 John was locked up, like thousands before him, in Marshalsea Prison. "The sun has set upon me for ever," he cried as he was led away, a little over-doing it, as always.

Marshalsea Prison in Borough High Street in south London was an ugly rectangular building broken up into a number of crowded and smelly houses. It was surrounded by a narrow pavement hemmed in by high, spiked walls. Now, in the evening, after a day at Warren's, Charles would make the hour-long trek to visit his father. The first time, he turned up at the main gate and was directed to the guard house where John was waiting to take him up to his room. On the second to top storey, it was actually no more than a cell, three metres long by four metres wide, with a window out of which you could see the sky but not the street. They sat before a small brick fire and father and son were soon in tears. "Take a warning by the Marshalsea," John urged his boy. "If a man had twenty pounds a year and spent nineteen pounds nineteen shillings and sixpence, he would be happy; but a shilling spent the other way would make him wretched." At ten o'clock, the bell rang and Charles left with the other visitors. Deeply depressed, he weaved his way through the dangerous streets back home.

The other Dickenses remained in Gower Street for a few weeks, but at the beginning of April, with most of their possessions sold, Elizabeth and the younger children moved into the Marshalsea with John, where, at least, they would not go hungry. Fanny remained at the Royal Academy studying music on a scholarship while Charles lodged with a friend of the family in a street near their last home. Now he really was alone. Abandoned. Almost, he felt, an orphan. He shared a room but had to prepare his own breakfast from a small loaf of bread and a mug of milk. In a cupboard he kept on a particular shelf another loaf and a portion of cheese to have as his supper.

On Sundays, his day off from the blacking factory, he would pick up his sister from the academy and together they would join the rest of the family in the jail. Charles was brave. Only once, about three weeks into his new life, did he complain bitterly about his life. He was a boy who was used to keeping his feelings hidden and, if the outburst did not make him feel any better, it at least had the effect of waking his parents up to how unhappy he was. As a result, Charles was found a new place to lodge just two minutes' walk from the prison. The landlord and landlady were plump, kindly people and, although Charles's room was once again an attic, it had a pleasant view. Best of all, the new arrangements meant he could visit his family for breakfast and supper.

But life in the factory was as unpleasant as ever. Of course, a lively spirit cannot be entirely crushed by circumstances. Not every day was terrible. His mother would visit sometimes and he soon found himself getting on better with the other boys, who liked him because he was so good at telling stories. After work they would sometimes play together on the coal barges. Sensibly, he decided to do his work, dull as it was, as well as he could and so discovered the pleasure in performing simple tasks properly. He was also earning money. On Saturday nights, he would walk home with six shillings in his pocket feeling quite grown up and during the following week could spend some of it in cake and coffee shops. Once he went to a pub and asked for "your very best – the VERY *best* – ale". The barlady, guessing his age, poured him one and gave him a kiss to go with it.

But not even the good days could take away the shame he felt about his life now. One afternoon at work he was suddenly struck by that old pain in his side and the seizure was so severe that he rolled on to the floor. Bob Fagin made up a bed of straw in the office and filled empty blacking bottles with hot water to use as hot water bottles. When Charles felt a bit better, Bob offered to walk him home to his parents. There was a problem, however. Charles had not told his friends that his father was in jail. So when they got near Southwark Bridge, Charles pretended that he lived in a house nearby. He waved Bob away and, fearing he might look back, knocked at a complete stranger's home. When a woman opened the door, Charles puzzled her by asking if Robert Fagin lived there.

The fact was John Dickens's spirits were recovering far faster than his son's. Cheerful and talkative, he was elected chairman of the prisoners' committee. Among his jobs was organizing a petition begging the king, George IV, to grant the prisoners drinking money so that they could toast His Majesty's health on his birthday. Charles was there as the inmates lined up to sign it and he amused himself by making up an imaginary life history for each of them.

On 26th April, John Dickens's mother died. She left him four hundred and fifty pounds. With this money now on its way, John's brother William paid off the baker's debt. A court hearing was called and Charles was summoned so the court could work out how much his clothes – such as his white hat – were worth in case they needed to be sold. It was another humiliation but at least it was now agreed that John could leave prison and pay a sum each month in order to clear his remaining debts. On May 28, after fourteen weeks in Marshalsea Prison, John was released and the family moved in with Charles.

Charles naturally, but wrongly, imagined that his factory days were over. Although his father was back at work, money was still short. Things *were* better, however. His mother now prepared him a lunch which he carried to work tied up in a handkerchief. The blacking firm was proving a success and had moved to lighter, less ramshackle premises in Covent Garden. Charles and Bob Fagin had become so good at their jobs that they were put to work in the window as a kind of advertisement. At the end of the year the family moved back to Camden. It meant Charles now had to walk five miles to work and five back, but walking was something he never minded and the family was together in its own home.

Yet inside he still felt slighted. Fanny had done so well at music college that she had won two prizes. With the rest of the family, Charles went to see her collect them. That night he went to bed feeling more neglected than ever. He would never know the kind of success his sister was experiencing! Not, of course, he said to himself, that he was jealous – Charles could never bear to think himself in the wrong.

In later life he could not remember how long his time at Warren's lasted. He thought it might have been at least a year. It was probably less than six months. When it ended, it ended suddenly. His father was passing Warren's one day and saw Charles in the window. Suddenly he understood the shame his son had felt for so long. This was not what a gentleman's son should be seen doing! He demanded to see James Lamert and told him he would not put up with Charles being made a public spectacle. James was annoyed. After all, he had only taken him on as a favour. The men argued and James said the boy would have to leave. It was very nasty and although Charles desperately wanted to go he did not want to be fired, let alone to the sound of his boss calling his father names.

Back home his mother thought her husband was being stupid. Who knew how long John would keep his job? There were debts to pay. So she went to see James, apologised, and he agreed to take Charles back. When she returned to tell him the "good" news, Charles was horrified. Luckily, his father's pride prevented the boy's return to the factory. Still, despite always loving his mother, Charles never truly forgave her for what she did. "I never shall forget," he wrote, "never can forget that my mother was warm [keen] for me being sent back."

Charles soon got his wish and was sent to school.

The days of prison and the blacking factory were over except that when something so painful happens to you when you are young, it is never really over. For the rest of his life, Charles was haunted by the fear of poverty and he worked hard, exhaustingly hard, to make sure he was never poor again, never afraid to argue with publishers if he felt they were not paying him enough. But he did not tell anyone about this period in his life, not even his wife and children. They knew nothing of it until after he had died. The secret became such an old one that it grew into part of him – and a part of his novels. Again and again Charles Dickens would write stories about bright children left alone to survive in a brutal world.

CHAPTER FOUR
The Poor Boy Becomes a
Wealthy Gentleman

So, at the age of twelve, Charles left Warren's and joined Wellington House Academy in north London as a day boy. None of his fellow pupils had any idea of what he had just been through. He looked healthy enough and, although small, he held himself well with a straight back. There was an air of smartness about him and he was happy to let people imagine that he really was the son of a gentleman. It was not a particularly good school. It was owned, he later said, by the most ignorant and bad tempered man he had ever met; but a school it was, and there he learned English grammar, Latin, history and geography and the violin. His friends noticed how he would often laugh very hard at nothing in particular. He was happy again. Like his father, Charles could never be laid low for very long. In 1827, now aged fifteen, he left for a job as a clerk in a lawyer's office. There he learned shorthand, a skill he needed for his next job which was reporting Parliament for a newspaper. It was a more hopeful time for him. He went to the theatre every night and for a while intended to be an actor. On one occasion he even planned to go to an audition but a bad cold meant he missed the chance.

In the summer of 1833, when he was twenty-one, he was rejected once and for all by a girl he had fallen in love with called Maria Beadnell. To take his mind off her, he began a short story, *A Dinner at Poplar Walk*. He needed cheering up, so it was a funny story. It began: "Mr Augustus Minns was a bachelor, of about forty as he said – of about eight-and-forty, as his friends said." Mr Minns worked (as John Dickens had) as a clerk in Somerset House and the story was about a proud family with money worries. Charles wrote it out on a single large piece of paper and one evening dropped it into the letter-box of a small publication called the *Monthly Magazine*. The next month he picked up the magazine – and there was his story! He walked down towards Westminster crying with joy and pride. He wrote another and then some more, using the name Boz. In 1836 the stories were collected in a volume under the title *Sketches by Boz* and that April he began publishing a long-running story, the *Pickwick Papers* concerning the adventures of Samuel Pickwick, "founder and general chairman of the Pickwick Club".

The same month, having by now got over Maria, he married the daughter of a newspaper editor he knew. Catherine Hogarth looked a bit like Maria, pretty and plump with heavy lidded blue eyes, but she was sweeter and less difficult than Maria had been. The following January they had a son, Charles, the first of ten children whom Catherine would give birth to at a rate of almost one a year, at great cost to her health and spirits.

So now, at not quite twenty-five, Charles was a husband and a father. He was also on the brink of becoming very famous. There was no doubt whatever about that. And famous he would remain – so famous that although some books were more popular than others and although he had his rivals and his critics, only Queen Victoria would be a more famous Victorian. No one helped him in this extraordinarily rapid rise from clerk to the greatest writer of his age and he asked for no one's help. Perhaps that was because he had received so little as a child.

He was a natural writer but he worked hard at it. He would lock himself in his study for five hours at a time, sometimes scribbling with great excitement if a story was going well, sometimes looking out of the window waiting for an idea. But even when his words came easily, he thought constantly about how he could make them better. The sheets of light blue paper on which he wrote in dark blue or black ink were full of crossings out and second thoughts, and the changes only became more frequent as he grew older and more expert in his craft.

Generally, he worked alone. Just once, though, his eldest daughter, Mamie, happened to be on hand to watch. She had been ill and Charles had allowed her this particular morning to stay on the sofa in his study. Suddenly, she was startled by him leaping from his chair and rushing to the mirror where he began to make faces. He raced back to his desk and wrote some more and then ran back to the mirror to pull faces again. He turned towards Mamie – but it was as if she was not there – for he began talking rapidly in a low voice. It seems that the would-be actor, who often starred in amateur dramatics with his friends, was performing the scenes in his books even before he wrote them down.

He was usually at work on at least two projects at once, sometimes two big novels at the same time. As well as writing, he edited other people's work. For a very short time, just eighteen days, he was actually the editor of a daily newspaper and for twenty years he edited magazines, *The Household Words* and then *All The Year Round*. He told his writers what he had no need to tell himself: that they should imagine their readers as intelligent, pleasant "but rather afraid of being bored".

Charles's own fear of boredom made him restless. In their first five years of marriage he and Catherine had moved homes three times. Finding London in the summer hot and dusty they would rent summer houses in Broadstairs on the Kent coast, or go to a cottage in Petersham in Middlesex in those months. As a family, they travelled to the Isle of Wight, and to France and Belgium on holiday. When he was forty-one he took off for three months to Europe with his friends, the painter Augustus Egg and the novelist Wilkie Collins. Twice he visited America, once with Catherine when he was thirty and, twenty-five years later on a reading tour. Every outing for Charles was more than a holiday. It was an adventure, a chance to register something new. Seeing Paris for the first time, he remarked that he had seen such "novelty". It was as if he had grown a new head beside his old one.

Wherever he was, he walked, thinking little of covering fifteen or twenty miles in an afternoon. He took a view doctors might agree with today, that the hours spent at a desk should be equalled by those spent exercising. Walking was his way off blowing off his extra energy. It gave him private time to work out plots and think about his life. After his father died in March 1851, Charles could not sleep and took to walking the streets of London all night till dawn. The wild moon and clouds, he thought, were "as restless as an evil conscience in a tumbled bed". Perhaps, he was guiltily remembering the resentment he had felt towards his spendthrift father when he was alive.

But on the long walks he took through London he also saw the characters and streets he would soon be describing. One night, not long after his father's funeral, he walked to a police station in the centre of London and spent the night there, watching and listening to the drunks and villains in the cells. He was fascinated and amused by the parts of life most people turn their eyes away from. He kept a raven as a pet. He enjoyed the boisterous honking and bustling of pigs. On a visit to Paris he repeatedly visited the city's morgue, examining the faces of the dead who had been hauled out of the River Seine and laid out on marble.

Such a man could not fail to be interested in ghosts and, although he did not really believe in them, he attended many séances, a popular pastime of the day in which people would sit round a table in a darkened room and try to make contact with the dead. Once he heard of a rumour that a ghost was haunting a monument near his home in the country. Charles, his fifteen-year-old son, Frank, and one of Frank's school friends, duly set out with a double-barrelled gun to investigate. Suddenly there was a terrific noise, both human and "superhuman". They advanced cautiously and discovered... a sheep with a bad cough.

In these ill-lit and spooky times, Charles stood out brightly. He wore colourful jackets and waistcoats, large cravats fixed by pins encrusted with jewels. He was a dandy, forever admiring himself in the mirror and combing his hair, even at dinner parties. He made sure his conversation was equally bright and tidy. In public, he was always "on", making jokes, doing impressions, pretending to be outraged by some scandal. One of the names he gave himself was "Mr Sparkler". He sparkled too brightly for some.

Wilkie Collins, who although a decade younger was frequently exhausted by his friend's energy, once complained: "A man who can do nothing by halves appears to me to be a fearful man."

A man who can do nothing by halves is unlikely, however, to be a poor one and Charles's prodigious (to use one of his favourite words) capacity for work did, for all his worrying about money, make him wealthy. One Friday in 1856 – he always felt Friday, the day of his birth, to be his lucky day – he bought Gad's Hill Place, the big house he had seen as a boy on walks and which his father had joked he might one day own. Moving in was a fulfilment of all the great expectations that had seemed buried by those early years in London.

But although he was sometimes mocked for living in a grand style in big houses while writing about the poor and homeless, Charles genuinely never forgot the world he had so narrowly escaped. He was on the board of many charities that helped the poor and provided for their education. He campaigned for better housing and sanitation for them. When the desperate wrote to him, he would reply and, if he was satisfied that their stories were genuine, he would often meet and help them personally.

He also never forgot those days spent visiting his father in jail and on his travels he made a point of visiting prisons, regarding the conditions in which prisoners were kept as a sign of how civilised a country really was. On his first trip to America, he insisted on going round Philadelphia's Eastern Penitentiary and although the jail was new he was shocked by how the system he saw worked, with each prisoner condemned to his own cell without company. Years later he put Marshalsea Prison, his father's jail, into his novel *Little Dorrit*. Its heroine is born in the jail and becomes known, after her mother's death, as "the Child of the Marshalsea".

Dickens is often accused of sentimentality in his novels, that is of trying to move his readers through cheap effects, but it is important to know that in his politics he was not an over-emotional man. He was very practical. He believed the poor should be fed and educated in order that they could go on to help themselves. He believed that criminals should not only be locked up but punished by being set to work. Although when he was young he wrote articles condemning the death sentence, he later changed his mind and supported it (though was always against public hangings).

In 1848, the political philosopher Karl Marx published with a colleague a short book called *The Communist Manifesto*. Its idea that the power and wealth of the rich should be distributed equally among everyone had an amazing influence on the world in the next century. Marx admired Dickens and once said that he had told the world "more political and social truths than have been uttered by all the professional politicians, publicists and moralists put together". But Charles was not a Marxist or a communist. He simply believed the system that was in place could be made to work more humanely. For that he counted, not on politicians, whom he distrusted, but on the good will of the better off. It has been said Charles was more like Father Christmas than Karl Marx. Even that is being too kind to some of his views, which today we find shocking – his belief that black Africans were savages, for instance, and his prejudice against Jews which spoils some of his descriptions of Fagin in *Oliver Twist*.

At heart, however, he believed in treating others as you would wish to be treated. He was inspired by the life of Jesus Christ, whose story he retold in a book written for his own children, *The Life of Our Lord*. When he prayed with his children at night, the prayer he taught them went: "Hear our supplications [pleadings] on behalf of the poor, the sick, the destitute and the guilty, and grant Thy blessing on the diffusion [the spread] of increased happiness and knowledge among the great mass of mankind, that they may not be tempted to the commission of crimes which in want and man's neglect it is hard to resist."

CHAPTER FIVE

Oliver, Smike and All the
Other Orphans

Above all, Charles wished his family – and his family of readers – to remember unfortunate children. It is not hard to understand why, for he considered he had been one himself. Before he had finished *The Pickwick Papers*, he had decided to write a proper novel that would depict the terrible conditions in which some of Britain's children were raised. Its hero would be not a well-fed gentleman like Samuel Pickwick, but a boy, "a poor houseless, wandering boy, without a friend to help him, or a roof to shelter his head." His name would be Oliver Twist.

While Charles was working out the plot of *Oliver Twist*, the newspapers were full of the terrible effects of a law passed by Parliament in 1834, the same year, as it happened, that slavery was abolished. The purpose of the Poor Law Amendment Act was to tighten up the way the poor were looked after. At the time those who could not look after themselves – children without families, the sick, the elderly, the unemployable and the mentally ill – were put into workhouses where, as the name suggests, they would labour in return for somewhere to sleep and eat. These were awful enough places, but Earl Grey's Whig government decided they were not terrible enough. It was thought they were encouraging people to scrounge. Committees of worthy citizens were appointed to make life in their local workhouses tougher.

The results were appalling. On entering the workhouse married couples were separated. Inmates were not given time or room to exercise. Children under fourteen were beaten. The work the paupers were made to do was dull and hard: breaking up stones, crushing up bones or untwisting old ropes to make a coarse fibre used to plug holes in pipes. But the meanest aspect of the workhouse of all was what the paupers were given to eat. A thin porridge of oatmeal was offered three times a day, with an onion twice a week and half a bread roll on Sundays. *The Times* called the system an "appalling machine" for "wringing the hearts of forlorn widowhood, for refusing the crust to famished age, for imprisoning the orphan in workhouse dungeons and for driving to prostitution the friendless and unprotected girl".

One such workhouse orphan was Oliver Twist. Near the start of Charles's story, he is selected by the other starving boys to ask on their behalf for a second helping.

"What!" said the master at length in a faint voice.
"Please sir," replied Oliver, "I want some more."
The master aimed a blow at Oliver's head with the ladle.

The next day a notice is placed on the gate outside the workhouse offering a reward of five pounds to take the nine year old off its hands and into any sort of employment they wished. And from there Oliver's adventures begin.

Oliver Twist began being serialised in February 1837 and immediately gripped its readers. But a whole year passed before the last episode appeared in April 1838, and Charles had become interested in another institution that supposedly cared for neglected children: the so-called Yorkshire Schools. He and Hablot Browne, who drew the pictures for

The Pickwick Papers (he signed himself "Phiz" just as in his early days Charles wrote under the nickname "Boz"), decided to travel to Yorkshire to investigate a well-known scandal that no one had done anything to end.

These boarding schools set in remote hills and moors advertised in London for pupils. Unfeeling parents, step parents and guardians were delighted to be offered an easy way to get their children out of their hair. A particular advertisement that caught Charles's eye went: "YOUTH are carefully instructed in the English, Latin and Greek languages, Common and Decimal Arithmetic; Book-keeping, Mensuration, Surveying, Geometry and Navigation. No extra charged whatsover, Doctor's bills excepted. No vacations, except by the Parents' desire." The lack of holidays was, naturally, a big plus for the parents. Once there, the children were taught next to nothing – let alone navigation – and lived on rations as bad as the workhouse's.

One school in particular had come to public notice, Bowes Academy near the River Greta. It was run by a Mr William Shaw who in the 1820s had been taken to court by the parents of two children who had been so neglected and starved that they had gone blind. During the case, the court heard how the boys' supper had been nothing more than warm milk and bread often crawling with maggots. Five children slept to one flea-ridden bed. They had been frequently flogged. Ten children in all had gone blind and between 1810 and 1834, twenty-five boys had died at the school. Shaw lost the case but, remarkably, the school survived and Shaw had remained in charge. In fact the advertisement that Charles had seen was his.

One Tuesday morning in January 1838, Charles and Hablot set off for Yorkshire by slow coach to Grantham and then, after an overnight stop, continued to Greta Bridge. The next day the two went on to Barnard Castle and began asking around about the local schools. And so it was that they came face to face with the famous Mr Shaw. Charles said he was looking for a school on behalf of a widow who had a son she could not look after, but Shaw was suspicious. He may even have recognised the author of *Oliver Twist*. Charles did not see much of Shaw's school but he saw some of its pupils with their "pale and haggard faces, lank and bony features, children with the countenances of old men, deformities with irons upon their limbs." That afternoon he inspected the local churchyard's snow-covered graves. He found the tombs of thirty-eight boys who had died in the local schools. One was of a George Ashton Taylor who had died "suddenly" at William Shaw's on 13th April 1822, at the age of 19. The epitaph read: "Young reader, thou must die, but after this the judgement."

His grave set Charles imagining what George must have been like. Soon into his head came the idea of a boy called Smike, who would play a big part in his next novel, *Nicholas Nickleby*. In this book, Nicholas briefly teaches at a school very much like William Shaw's called Dotheboys Hall. It is run by the harsh-voiced, one-eyed, ignorant and violent Wackford Squeers whose initials, you may notice, are the same as William Shaw's. When Nicholas meets Smike at the school he is the age that George Taylor was when he died. Squeers keeps Smike as a slave since no one has paid his school fees for six years. When he tries to run away, Squeers beats him. He is a pathetic, half-witted lad but gentle and good natured and when Nicholas thrashes Squeers in a fight and saves Smike from further punishment, he follows him to London.

When this part of *Nicholas Nickleby* came out, at

least three Yorkshire schoolmasters were convinced Squeers was based on them. Shaw was driven out of business. It is said his wife died early of the shame and that their daughter, according to some a sweet woman, was mocked in the street. Whatever the truth, by 1846, only six years after *Nicholas Nickleby* was published, a school inspector failed to find a single school in Yorkshire in the least resembling Dotheboys Hall. What the law had failed to achieve, Charles, in a story, had brought about. Words can be powerful things, but it is as well to remember that other evils continued despite Charles's best efforts. Workhouses, for example, were not abolished until 1929, more than 90 years after the publication of *Oliver Twist*.

Smike is rescued in the book but not soon enough to prevent his early death. He is the first of many children to die in the pages of Charles's books. I mentioned in the first chapter the public grief caused by the death of Little Nell in *The Old Curiosity Shop*, the book that followed *Nicholas Nickleby*. There would be many more. In *Dombey and Son*, Paul Dombey, a frail child dies peacefully in his sister's arms, and his death caused another outcry. In *David Copperfield*, David's wife Dora, his "child-wife", dies after giving birth to a still-born child. In a later book still, *Bleak House*, he writes about a road-sweeper called Jo, who was based on a real fourteen year old he had read about in a magazine who made a small living sweeping mud and horse manure from the streets and was so ignorant he had never heard of God. In *Bleak House*, Jo dies while saying the Lord's Prayer.

Some readers objected to these children's deaths and Charles himself knew it might look as if he was being cruel. For some, the emotions the deaths released were just too great. Others thought them sentimental, even ridiculous; a generation later, the playwright Oscar Wilde joked that it would take a heart of stone not to laugh at the death of Little Nell. Yet in the Nineteenth Century children did very often die. Charles's sister Fanny, for example, gave birth to a disabled child called Henry whom Charles was very fond of. He based Paul Dombey on the boy and, tragically, Henry died not long after *Dombey and Son* was completed.

A bitter memory from the early days of his marriage had particularly affected his thinking about the frailty of young women. After their wedding he and Catherine moved to 48 Doughty Street in

Bloomsbury, just north of the centre of London. (The house is now a Dickens museum.) Catherine had a younger sister called Mary, then just fifteen years old, and it was decided she should move in as a companion to Catherine. She soon became a sister to Charles too. Catherine did not find pregnancy easy: she miscarried several times and even after successful births became depressed. Mary's cheerfulness was particularly important to Charles as he worked away on *Pickwick* and *Oliver Twist*.

On 6th May 1837, the three of them, Charles, Catherine and Mary went to the theatre to see a comedy called *Is She His Wife?* and returned to Doughty Street at about one in the morning. Mary went up to her room in "her usual delightful spirits", but before she could undress, she cried out and collapsed. Her mother was called and Catherine and Charles sat up next to her all night. At three in the afternoon, she died in Charles's arms. The doctor said it was of heart disease. She was just seventeen.

Charles was deeply affected by this tragedy. He cut off a lock of Mary's hair and kept it in a special case and took a ring from her finger to wear. Every night for the next nine months he dreamed of the dead girl and, from time to time, for the rest of his life. There was no disloyalty to Catherine in this; it was like a brother's love, or, as he said, "a father's pride". He wrote: "From the day of our marriage the dear girl had been the grace and life of our home, our constant companion, and the sharer of our little pleasures." When, thirteen years later, he came to write of the death of Dora Copperfield it was Mary he was still thinking about.

Around the time he was writing her death scene, his wife gave birth to a girl they decided to call Dora. Eight months later, in April 1851, Charles spent the afternoon carrying little Dora around on his back and playing with his children in the garden. In the evening Charles went to speak at a charity event. After the speeches were over, one of his oldest friends, John Forster, took him aside. An hour before he had received a message that little Dora had suffered a fit and died. Charles with his usual self control said little and left immediately for home to sit beside his dead daughter. A few nights later, however, when some flowers had arrived in Dora's memory he "suddenly gave way completely".

The sad fact was that in Charles's day dying young was not the rarity it is today. In 1839, almost half the funerals in London were of children under ten. But if the deaths of children were common, it did not make any of them less heartbreaking. It was also much more common for women to die in childbirth and for parents to die young generally. Dickens's novels are crowded with orphans, but so was Britain. It was a reality Charles found hard to bear.

Charles helped children in every practical way he could. When Queen Victoria came to the throne in 1837 Britain headed a vast empire across the world that made many people very rich. Yet so many of them looked away or convinced themselves that in some strange sense the poor, even poor children, deserved to be poor – not so Charles, who had no qualms about picking up and comforting the filthiest child he might come across in his walks around London. In Boston on his first trip to America he made a point of visiting the Perkins School for The Blind. There he met a girl called Laura Bridgeman who, although deaf, dumb and blind, had been taught to communicate by touch. When he left he donated the equivalent of £100,000 in today's money so that his novels could be printed in raised texts for the blind.

One of his favourite charities was the Hospital for Sick Children in Great Ormond Street in London, which exists to this day (and is still in need of funds).

In 1858 he made a speech about children that was so powerful that it moved his audience to give more than £3,000 (the equivalent of £200,000 today) to the hospital. A few weeks later, to raise even more for it, he once again read in public *A Christmas Carol*.

CHAPTER SIX
Tiny Tim Who Did NOT Die

Perhaps this is the occasion we talked about in the prologue when we left Charles Dickens about to read *A Christmas Carol*. Let us imagine, then, that he is in London, not to make money for himself but to raise funds for Great Ormond Street.

"Marley was dead," he begins. He barely needs to look at his text. The story is already fifteen years old. Many in the audience can probably recite it word for word too.

I wonder if, even all this time later, I need to explain the story of *A Christmas Carol*. The story has never stopped being told. In America in the 1930s, a time of great unemployment, families would listen to it on Christmas Day performed by a famous actor, Lionel Barrymore, who would arrive in full make-up even though it was a radio broadcast. Sixty years later, as many fell in love with *The Muppet Christmas Carol*. You may have seen another film of it, or a stage production, or read a shortened version. Perhaps you have read the masterpiece itself. If you know the story and do not need to be reminded of it, feel free not to read this chapter. If you do not know it, you might want to skip on in any case – the last thing I want is to spoil your enjoyment when you do read the story.

But, if that leaves anyone still reading, here is what happens in *A Christmas Carol*.

It is late afternoon on a frosty, foggy Christmas Eve in old London and we are in the warehouse of a financial firm called Scrooge & Marley. Seven years ago to the day, Jacob Marley died – there is no doubt whatever about that – so now Ebenezer Scrooge runs the business alone. Oh, but Scrooge is a tight-fisted old man, "a squeezing, wrenching, grasping, scraping, clutching, covetous old sinner"! His cold heart has nipped his pointy nose and turned his thin lips blue. In his counting house, he pores over his accounts. In the room beyond works his loyal and badly paid clerk Bob Cratchit.

Before he closes up for the night, Scrooge is troubled by visitors. The first is his cheerful nephew,

Fred, who makes the mistake of wishing his uncle a merry Christmas. "Bah!" says Scrooge. "Humbug!" Why should Fred be merry? He is poor. Fred asks why Scrooge should be so miserable, for he is rich. Angrily, his uncle turns down the young man's invitation to join his family for Christmas dinner the next day. After that, two portly gentlemen turn up explaining they are collecting for the poor, thousands of whom do not have enough to eat at this time of year. Scrooge chases them away, saying sarcastically he had not heard the workhouses had closed. Finally, it is time to lock up. Bob Cratchit snuffs out the candle that he works by and Scrooge sniffs that he supposes Bob will be wanting Christmas Day off *and* expect to be paid for it. "It is only once a year," Bob points out miserably.

After dinner alone in his usual pub, Scrooge makes his way to his home, a set of gloomy rooms that had once belonged to Marley. It is a funny thing, but as he turns his key in the lock, he thinks he sees the door knocker turn into Marley's face, a face with a dismal light about it, "like a bad lobster in a cellar". Scrooge ignores it, and climbs the dark stairs to his rooms. He changes into his dressing gown, slippers and night cap and takes his porridge off the stove for supper. Because he is so mean, he has lit only a very low fire and has to sit close to it on this cold night. Again it is strange: the tiles around the grate all seem to have become pictures of Marley's head. "Humbug," Scrooge says again, but shortly afterwards there is a ringing of bells and a clanging of chains as if someone, or something, is dragging itself upstairs. The ghost of Jacob Marley enters the room. He is wearing his old clothes, but beneath his bandaged face, his body is completely see-through.

"You don't believe in me," suggests Marley's ghost and Scrooge agrees he does not. He is just seeing things, probably because of something he has eaten, an undigested bit of beef or a crumb of cheese. "Humbug!" he says, but, at this insult, Marley's ghost unwraps its bandage and its jaw drops off. Scrooge falls to his knees in terror and admits, yes, he does believe in him. Marley explains that when he was alive his spirit never walked beyond the "narrow limits of our money-changing hole". As punishment, it is now condemned to wander the world in chains. But, Scrooge objects, why should Marley be punished for being a good businessman. "Business!" the ghost wails. "Mankind was my business." And this is why Marley has paid Scrooge a visit. It may still not be too late for Scrooge to avoid his dead partner's fate – *if* he learns the lessons that will be taught him this night. The ghost floats out through the window. "Hum—" says Scrooge, but he does not have the heart to finish the word. He falls asleep on his bed.

When he wakes it is still dark. In fact, when he hears the local church's chimes, he discovers it is midnight again. He goes back to bed. Unable to sleep, he hears the clock strike one. Suddenly the room lights up and the curtains of his four-poster bed are drawn aside. A strange being stands before him, something with a boy's face and old man's body and with a beam of light shooting up from its scalp. "I am the Ghost of Christmas Past," it announces. "Your past."

He leads Scrooge out of bed, through the walls, into the night, and on to an open country road. Scrooge realises he was brought up near here. Into his old schoolhouse they go, and Scrooge looks upon himself as a lonely child reading, while outside his classmates are out having fun. "Poor boy," cries Scrooge. Then he sees his own sister, Fanny, darting through the door. She has come to take him home: "Home for good and all. Home for ever and ever.

Father is so much kinder than he used to be, that home's like Heaven."

Next the Ghost of Christmas Past takes old Scrooge back to his first place of work. It is an office run by a jolly gentleman named Fezziwig who is telling his young employees to put their pens down. It is Christmas Eve and there is to be a party. A splendid party it is too, with beer and food and dancing and music and all the pretty Fezziwig daughters! The ghost says the party does not cost Fezziwig very much. Scrooge replies that this is not the point: "The happiness he gives is quite as great as if it cost a fortune."

They are off again and now Scrooge sees himself as a young man talking to a girl who is breaking off her engagement with him. They had promised to marry when they were both poor. Now Scrooge is well off but seems to prefer money to her. "May you be happy in the life you have chosen," she says. Old Scrooge cannot bear this memory and shouts to the spirit: "Show me no more." But the Ghost takes him to the family she went on to have with another man. They see her husband return home to be greeted by his daughter and hear him say to his wife that he saw an old friend of hers today, Ebenezer Scrooge: "Quite alone in the world, I do believe." Old Scrooge seizes the ghost's cap and pulls it all the way down over its frail body. The ghost vanishes and Scrooge is back in his bed.

Once more, the church bell strikes one. A ghostly light blazes in from the sitting room. When Scrooge investigates he finds the room has been transformed into a happy Christmas scene, full of holly and ivy with turkeys and plum puddings covering the floor. "I am the Ghost of Christmas Present," says a cheery giant dressed in a green robe and with icicles on its head. "Touch my robe," it commands and suddenly the two of them are on a city street on a bustling Christmas morning. People are carrying their dinners to the baker's shop (where it was customary for the poor to have their food cooked in the big oven on Sundays and holidays). Scrooge is led to Bob Cratchit's humble home where Mrs Cratchit and the many Cratchit children are waiting for Bob to come back from church. He arrives with another son on his shoulder, Tiny Tim. Alas Tiny Tim is not well and walks with a crutch. But the family is soon excitedly devouring its goose and mashed potatoes, and then its Christmas pudding. "A Merry Christmas to us all my dears. God bless us," says Bob raising a glass.

Tiny Tim, his withered little hand in his father's, adds: "God bless us, everyone."

"Spirit," says Scrooge, "tell me if Tiny Tim will live."

"I see a vacant seat in the poor chimney corner," the Ghost replies, "and a crutch without an owner, carefully preserved. If these shadows remain unaltered by the Future, the child will die."

"No, no," says Scrooge. "Oh, no kind Sprit! Say he will be spared."

Then Bob, much to his wife's disgust, proposes a toast to Scrooge. A torture though these scenes are to Scrooge, the ghost has not done with him yet. Soon he is standing with him on a bleak moor where a miner's family is singing a carol. Next, they travel over rough seas to a lighthouse where the keepers are having a rough-and-ready Christmas dinner together. Then they visit a ship. Although the sailors are far from home, each makes sure to say a kind word to his mates on this special night. Everyone it seems knows how to celebrate Christmas except for Scrooge.

Suddenly, Scrooge hears his nephew's laugh and discovers himself in Fred's sitting room just as Fred is telling the family how his strange uncle thinks Christmas is humbug. Everyone says they have no time for the old man but Fred says he feels sorry for him. "Who suffers by his ill whims? Himself, always." The family soon forgets the topic and begins a round of dances and games. They have to guess the name of the growling, grunting animal that lives in London. The answer is "Ebenezer Scrooge" and, by now, old Scrooge looking on is so caught up in their high spirits he doesn't mind the joke.

And still their trip continues, through poor bleak lands and hospitals and jails. Scrooge notices that the ghost is getting older and older and, also, that four little feet are now sticking out of the bottom of its robe. From within emerge two miserable children. The ghost explains:

"This boy is Ignorance. This girl is Want. Beware them both, and all of their degree, but most of all beware this boy, for on his brow I see that written which is Doom."

The clock strikes twelve. The ghost is gone but another phantom approaches, so draped and hooded that it is impossible to make out its shape, face or anything but an outstretched hand. It does not speak but Scrooge knows it must be the Ghost of Christmas Yet To Come. It takes him to the City of London where merchants are discussing a colleague who has just died and who will not be missed. Scrooge shivers and wonders what this dead man has to do with him. Before long they move to a part of town which Scrooge has heard of but never been to. The streets are foul and narrow; the shops and houses wretched, the people half naked, drunken, slipshod, ugly. In a particular shop some lowly tradesmen are sorting through the belongings of someone recently dead. "I hope he didn't die of anything catching," says one. "Spirit," says Scrooge shuddering, "I see. I see. The case of this unhappy man *might* be my own."

Scrooge is led to the deathbed of this lonely man. "If there is any person in the town who feels emotion caused by this man's death show that person to me," Scrooge asks, but the only people the ghost can find who show any reaction to the death are a desperate family who had owed the dead man money, and are pleased they no longer need to repay it. Back in the Cratchit household, the ghost and Scrooge notice Tiny Tim's empty chair. Bob tries to be brave but breaks down at the thought of his dead boy.

"Spectre," asks Scrooge, "tell me what man that was whom we saw lying dead." The ghost takes him past the window of his office where another man now works, and then on to a graveyard. On a tombstone

Scrooge reads his own name: EBENEZER SCROOGE. He falls upon the ground and begs to be told that the future can be changed. "I will honour Christmas in my heart, and try to keep it all the year. I will live in the Past, the Present and the Future." But the ghost only shrinks and dwindles down into a bedpost.

It is, Scrooge realises to his huge relief, his own bedpost. And it's morning at last. He scrambles out of bed feeling as merry as a schoolboy. As he hears the church bells ring, he runs to the window and shouts to a passing boy: "What's today, my fine fellow?" "Why, Christmas Day," the boy replies and Scrooge gives him money to go to the butchers where a prize turkey is on sale. The turkey, so big it could never have stood up, is promptly sent to the Cratchits. Scrooge dresses up in his best clothes and rushes into the streets smiling and wishing everyone Merry Christmas. He even runs into the charity collectors and surprises them by promising to give them a very large sum of money indeed. He goes to church, talks to beggars, and finally ends up at Fred's. "It's I," he announces. "Your Uncle Scrooge. I have come to dinner. Will you let me in, Fred?" And, of course, he is very welcome.

The next day Scrooge is determined to arrive in his office before Bob Cratchit. When Bob turns up, a little befuddled from the previous day's celebrations, eighteen and a half minutes late, Scrooge says he will not stand for it and, therefore... "Therefore I am about to raise your salary – I'll raise your salary and endeavour to assist your struggling family..."

The book concludes:

Scrooge was better than his word. He did it all and infinitely more and to Tiny Tim, who did NOT die, he was a second father. He became as good a friend, as good a master, and as good a man, as the good old city knew, or any other good old city, town or borough in the good old world.

CHAPTER SEVEN
The Invention of Christmas

When in these readings of *A Christmas Carol*, Charles came to the line "and to Tiny Tim, who did NOT die", his audiences often whooped with joy. In a period when sick children often did die, and from an author who was not afraid to let the children in his books die, this was Dickens's Christmas present to his public. It is a kind of miracle. In the chapter about the Ghost of Christmas Yet To Come, Tiny Tim appears to have died. But at the end he comes back to life. All this is in a novelist's power.

Charles did this sort of thing more than once. Riding in his carriage in Regent's Park in London one day, for example, he accidentally ran over a girl's dog. He was very upset and in his next novel, *Dombey and Son*, he brought the dog back as Flora

Dombey's pet Diogenes, "as ridiculous a dog as one would meet with on a summer's day".

A *Christmas Carol* was not the only story he wrote especially for Christmas, although it was the first, the most popular and the best. Each of them is a ghost story of sorts. They feature goblins, fairies, spirits and, in one, a talking cricket who lives in the fireplace. Each one includes children, poor people and someone who has lost touch with his better side. In each, also, there are frequent mentions of clocks and time passing. What there is not much mention of is Jesus. Nevertheless, Charles insisted that his Christmas books expressed thoughts "taken from the lips of Christ". Charles was a Christian who was not very interested in heaven and angels but very much interested in the lessons Jesus taught about how we should live while we are in this world.

It was Jesus of course who invented Christmas – then again, that's not totally true either. Long before the first Christians appeared, the Romans used to celebrate the shortest day of the year with drinking, music and presents, all in honour of one of their gods, Saturn (the festival was called Saturnalia). In Ancient Britain there were also great feasts and celebrations held in the middle of winter. They were there to cheer people up in the darkest part of the year, a way of making fun of the evil forces that had stripped the trees of their leaves and stopped the crops from growing. Food saved from the summer would be eaten: boar's head, pigs, turkeys and geese. Then in the Fourth Century when the early Christians were keen to convert Europe to their God, they cleverly introduced the story of Christ's miraculous birth into the partying, as if it was all their idea in the first instance.

The Normans, who invaded Britain in 1066, coined the word "Christ-Masse". Their kings enjoyed outdoing one another with the size of their celebrations over the twelve days of the holiday. New traditions were added to old. By Queen Elizabeth I's time, wassailers sang on the porches of houses and were invited in to drink punch from a big bowl; and from this developed carol singing. In 1644, the event had become such a party that a group of religious killjoys called the Puritans passed a law banning it and declared 25th December to be a day of prayer and fasting. Few laws were so unpopular or so quickly abolished.

By the time Charles was growing up in the early nineteenth century the tradition of giving presents and spoiling children was well established, as was kissing under the mistletoe and all the Christmas games that involved touching and kissing. The Victorians, living during the reign of a queen who dressed permanently in black after she was widowed, loved Christmas even more than we do perhaps because the rest of the year they were expected to be strict and proper. It was in their era that Christmas crackers were first made and that the German tradition of the Christmas tree became popular after Queen Victoria and her German husband, Prince Albert, were pictured in a magazine standing next to theirs.

So, you might say, what was there left for Dickens to add? Yet in some very real ways he invented the Christmas we know today. For one, nothing is ever truly invented until it has been properly recorded and before Charles Dickens's *A Christmas Carol*, English Christmas had not yet been described so brilliantly. It is true that Walter Scott, the great Scottish novelist who died in 1832, wrote accounts of Christmas in his history novels, but these were about celebrations held by the rich in great halls, not the Christmases of people like the Cratchits or Fezziwigs. It was left to Charles Dickens to capture the boisterous comedy of the British in a mood of over-the-top indulgence.

Charles was, actually, not a big eater, but he loved describing food and seemed to find it comical. *A Christmas Carol* contains long lists of Christmas treats: "sucking-pigs, long wreaths of sausages, mince-pies, plum-puddings, barrels of oysters, red-hot chestnuts" and on and on – not forgetting the turkey so fat it could not stand up. There is plenty to drink too in his stories, not all of it liquid: in *The Cricket on the Hearth*, a baby is handed around at Christmas "as if it were something to drink". The writer G K Chesterton later wrote of Dickens that "he devoted his genius in a somewhat special sense to the description of happiness".

As well as enjoying describing Christmas, Charles loved celebrating it. It was the time of year when the Victorians – who were known for thinking children should be seen and not heard – put their children first and, as we know, he loved children. In an essay he wrote in 1850 called *The Christmas Tree*, Charles stares at "that pretty German toy", the Christmas tree, and describes everything hanging on it, from toy watches to jewels, from wooden apples to dolls who when you took their heads off turned out to be made of sugar plums. He hears a young child whisper to a friend: "There was everything and more." He would take his own children to a toyshop in London and the salesman who demonstrated the latest toys would find Charles was just as a keen to try them out as his sons and daughters. On Twelfth Night, the last day of Christmas, Charles would direct his children in a play in which, of course, he took the starring role. Afterwards there would be a party to celebrate its success.

Nevertheless, he was tense and anxious when he wrote *A Christmas Carol*. He knew he had a good story but walked through the streets at night worrying he might let it down in the writing. When he finally got to "The End" – and underlined the words three times – he knew it was not just Scrooge's turn to celebrate but his own. "Such dinings, such dancings, such conjurings, such blind-man's bluffings, such theatre-goings, such kissings-out of old years and kissings-in of new ones," he wrote. "I broke out like a mad-man."

Yet the heart of *A Christmas Carol* is not the Fezziwigs' Ball. It is those two children, Ignorance and Want. The poor, it is sometimes said, are always with us, and they are with us throughout *A Christmas Carol*. What Charles was saying was that it is not enough just to remember those left outside in the cold. That could leave us feeling cosy and smug. We should do something to *help* them. The Christmas spirit, he wrote, is "the spirit of active usefulness, perseverance, cheerful discharge of duty, kindness and forbearance". Charles's Christmas stories were one of the treats of Christmas, but each contained a serious moral.

The first to follow *A Christmas Carol* was *The Chimes*, a "goblin story" about a kindly man called Trotty Veck who stands outside a church waiting for people to give him messages to deliver. On New Year's Eve he has a dream about the sort of terrible world it would be if politicians and judges continued to show no sympathy to the poor. Charles wrote it, he said, not warmed by Christmas cheer but blazing away, "wrathful and hot". The moral of *The Cricket on the Hearth*, his next Christmas book, pointed to the importance of being truthful with those we love. The Christmas after he followed it with *The Battle for Life*, about a family that is almost torn apart because two sisters love the same man. Christmas, he concludes, should be a time of "great forgiving".

It is also a time to remember. Charles's last Christmas book, published in 1849, is called *The Haunted Man and The Ghost's Bargain* and is about a man with such sad memories of his past that he does a deal with a ghost to have them erased. But without his memory of the wrongs done against him, the clever chemist finds he has forgotten the lessons they taught him and that he has lost his ability to be kind towards others. "Lord," it ends, "Keep my Memory Green." It seems that Charles was thinking about his own memories of his childhood, for at around this time he wrote a private account of his youth that he wanted to be published after his death.

Then a few years later, when he was not quite forty, he wrote a touching essay called *What Christmas Is, As We Grow Older*. In it he tells us to remember and learn from those who have died. It was composed at the end of the year in which he had lost his baby daughter Dora and it also recalls his long dead sister-in-law Mary – "almost a woman, never to be one" – and Harry, his crippled nephew, the model for Paul Dombey and, perhaps, Tiny Tim.

And what of Tiny Tim, who did NOT die? *A Christmas Carol* was, in a way, written on his behalf and on behalf of children who suffered as he did. The year before, a shocking Parliamentary report had been published into the "Employment and Condition of Children in Mines and Manufactories". That

October, Charles went down a Cornish tin mine where children as young as five were made to work. He was outraged by what he saw and determined to strike a "sledge-hammer blow" on behalf of these children. The sledgehammer was *A Christmas Carol*.

In 1848 Parliament passed an act banning women and children from working underground in mines and, during the rest of his life, Charles saw the gradual ending of child labour altogether. He would not claim to be responsible, for it required politicians and lawyers to sit down and write new laws. But it also required a new way of thinking about children and about the poor. *A Christmas Carol* went a long way to making people think differently. When he read the story in America, a factory owner was so moved that he closed his factories on Christmas Day. It is a small example but Lord Jeffrey, the old judge who cried at the deaths in Charles's books, declared that with *A Christmas Carol* his friend had "done more good, and not only fostered more kindly feelings, but promoted more positive acts of beneficence, by this little publication than can be traced to all the pulpits of Christendom, since [the previous] Christmas."

CHAPTER EIGHT
The Last Singing of the Carol

Let us take another look at Charles. It is 15th March 1870, and although he is still only fifty eight, he looks like an old man. His beard is white, his left hand is swollen and he walks with a limp. He has just finishing reading *A Christmas Carol* and is about to receive the most thunderous applause, for this is a special night. The crowds in St James's Hall in London know that, after sixteen years, this will be the last of his readings. After the cheering has finished, Charles makes a short speech. There is, he promises, another book to look forward to, a murder story called *The Mystery of Edwin Drood*. "But from these garish lights I vanish now for ever more, with a heartfelt, grateful, respectful and affectionate farewell." Charles has always prided himself on not showing emotion in public but now, as the applause starts again, tears fall down his lined face.

The unstoppable Charles Dickens was finally slowing to a halt. It was not a surprise to him or to his friends, for his health – which from childhood had always been unreliable – had worsened over the last few years. His reading tour of America had exhausted him and by the end his right foot was so enlarged he could not squeeze it into a boot. For his performance at the Steinway Hall in New York cards were slipped into the audience's programmes reading "Mr Charles Dickens begs indulgence for a Severe Cold, but hopes its effects may not be very perceptible after a few minutes Reading." They were not, but he was ill with more than a cold.

It was not just work that had sapped his energy. His personal life in the last fifteen years had become an unhappy mess. In early middle age Charles had realised he had married the wrong woman. After the first flush of love had passed, he found he had little to say to Catherine. He got on much better with her younger sister, Georgina – and indeed, in his memory, with Mary, the sister who had never been allowed to grow old. Catherine, meanwhile, was now middle-aged and overweight (just as he had become middle-aged and excessively thin). After all the children, she had grown tired and slow, unable to keep up with her husband's galloping conversation, let alone his galloping walks.

Even so, the marriage might have endured out of affection for the good times and for the children's sake, if Charles had not had a disastrous habit of falling in love. His crushes were always on much younger women, some of them scarcely more than girls. Mostly he kept his feelings to himself or confided them jokingly to friends.

When he was forty-five, however, he fell deeply for a pretty young actress, just eighteen years old, named Nelly Ternan who had been acting with him in the half-amateur, half-professional theatre troupe he sometimes took round the country. She enthralled him. He could think of nothing else. And before long Catherine had come to suspect something and confronted him. Charles acted as if he were outraged and denied there was anything wrong with his fondness for the girl, but the row did not blow over. One sleepless night in October 1857, he got up at two in the morning and walked out on Catherine – actually walked, some thirty miles all the way from London to Gad's Hill, his second home in Kent.

They got back together but there was a gloom

about the home and no party that Christmas. The following May Catherine discovered that Charles had given Nelly some jewellery. They argued again. This settled it. Charles demanded a legal separation and told Catherine she would have to leave Tavistock House, their home in London for the last seven years. Although he provided her with enough money to live in comfort, he never wanted to see her again. Instead he moved Nelly Ternan and her mother, Frances, also an actress, into a house just off the Hampstead Road. Later he paid for them to rent a house in France which he also visited frequently. Nelly sometimes stayed at Gad's Hill Place. Were they lovers? No one knows for certain but they probably were, at least for a time. In any case she split up his family.

Today marriages break up all the time but in the middle of the nineteenth century divorce was rare and scandalous. It is a surprise, really, and a tribute to his work, that once the early rumours had died down, the separation did not damage his fans' high regard for him. We must feel sorry for Charles, of course, feeling so trapped and unhappy in his marriage, but we must feel even sorrier for Catherine, who had given him everything she was capable of. It is sad that a man who believed in keeping families together should have ended up making his children choose between their loyalty to him and to their mother. It is a terrible thing too that Charles let it be known that he thought Catherine had been an unaffectionate mother – a charge which was simply untrue. After he died, his daughter Kate, who at the time had sided with him, said her father was not "a gentleman" and did not understand women. "My father was a wicked man – a very wicked man," she said, "but he was wonderful!"

It is not today's way to call people wicked – let alone people we have not met. Wonderful, however, we can agree upon – and not just in print but in person. He was amusing. He was witty. He did not mind being rude if he was also being funny. His sense of the absurd often sent him into giggles – even at funerals. He had a temper too, which when unleashed made him, it was said, "demoniacal", like a demon. His tantrums sound spectacular. Even his depressions were rather wonderful: sudden, deep, and then over. He was not as boring as most adults. In many ways, the boy who had been made to grow up so early always remained a boy.

He saw life as an adventure and sometimes he sought it out. On holiday in Italy when he was thirty-three, he insisted on leading Catherine and her sister Georgina up the side of Vesuvius by moonlight. The volcano was erupting but still he insisted on them climbing up, first on horseback then on foot. Finally they came to the base of the cone itself but even then Charles was not satisfied and clambered another few hundred feet until he was looking down into its "flaming bowels". He swigged a bottle of wine in celebration and scrambled down to join the others "alight in half a dozen places and burnt from head to foot". (Did I mention he exaggerated?)

Sometimes adventure sought him out. In the summer of 1865, Charles, now fifty-three, was returning from a holiday in Boulogne with Nelly and Mrs Ternan. They had arrived by ferry to Folkestone and were on the 2.39pm steam train to London. Charles enjoyed rail travel – he was always on the side of progress and novelty – and was enjoying the comforts of their first-class compartment when suddenly disaster befell them.

The railway line which crossed the bridge over the River Beult, just outside Staplehurst in Kent, was being repaired and the foreman had muddled up the train timetables. Not expecting a train for two hours, he was alarmed to look up and see Charles's engine approaching the bridge at fifty miles an hour. The train's driver had no idea that the tracks had been taken up. Frantically the signal man raised his red flag. The driver braked, but it was too late. The train jumped the gap where the tracks should have been and swerved off the bridge. Seven first-class carriages fell down to the riverbed. The eighth remained hanging from the bridge. In it, thrown into the corner, were Charles and Frances and Nelly Ternan.

The women screamed. Charles told them to be calm. "You may be sure nothing worse can happen. Our danger must be over," he reasoned. So they stayed still, while Charles climbed out of the window and saw the broken bridge. At that moment, two guards came running by. "Look at me," Charles commanded. "Do stop an instant and look at me, and tell me whether you don't know me." "We know you very well, Mr Dickens," said one of the men who was then happy to trust him with the keys to the compartment. Slowly Charles led the women up a plank and out of the upturned carriage to safety.

Only now did he see the carriages crumpled down below on the river bed. With great coolness, he re-entered the dangling carriage and removed his travelling brandy flask and top hat. With them in his hands, he clambered down the hill and began to tend the injured, the dying and the dead below. He gave them drops of brandy to drink and poured water, which he had collected from the river in his hat, over their faces. It was a tragic scene but he did everything he could before he left it.

He was about to rejoin the Ternans when he remembered that he had left the latest instalment of *Our Mutual Friend*, the book he was writing, in the carriage. So he returned to the swaying compartment yet again and rescued it. When he finally arrived on a rescue train at Charing Cross Station in London, he confessed he was "shattered and broken up". He had been brave at a moment of crisis but his nerves never fully recovered. Never again did the man who seemed always in motion – even if it was just the motion of his hand dashing across a page – take the same delight in travel.

Did life tire out Charles before he could grow old, or did he tire the life out of himself? Whichever was the case, by Christmas 1869, he was spent. His foot was swollen again and he was unable to make it down from his room in Gad's Hill for Christmas lunch. That evening, however, he could not resist the lure of party games and he was led down to join the party.

At first he just watched his family play, but when his favourite memory game started he joined in. The idea was to repeat the words said by the people before you and add some of your own until the sequence became too long and one by one the players gave up. Charles still had an excellent memory and, when his turn came, he remembered everybody's contributions exactly and then added some words of his own: "Warren's Blacking, thirty-three The Strand". We, of course, know they were the name and address of his old blacking factory but his children were puzzled. He had never mentioned that part of his life to them.

In June, a little short of three months after his final public reading, his sister-in-law Georgina was sitting down to dinner with him when she noticed that he was looking ill. "Yes, very ill. I have been very ill for the last hour," Charles said. Then he had some sort of fit and fell from her arms to the ground unconscious. A doctor came and a couch was brought into the room. Charles lay wrapped in rugs, his head supported by pillows. His daughters were called and they stayed up with him through the night but he did not regain consciousness. The next afternoon, with Nelly also by his side, at ten past six, Charles Dickens died. It was five years to the day since the train crash. In the garden *The Mystery of Edwin Drood* lay unfinished in the chalet where he worked.

When the news reached London, a flower girl asked: "Does this mean Father Christmas is dead?" It did not, but it did mean that the world would now have to read his books to itself. And so must we. To do so is to begin an adventure that, because he wrote so much, can last a lifetime. We discover that each story is, as he said of *Oliver Twist*, like "streaky, well cured bacon", full of changes of mood, scene, time and place. Like the man himself, the books move along quickly. Nevertheless, certain passages can still sometimes seem slow to us today. Don't worry about that. Once, when Dickens was travelling in America, he was recognised by a little girl on a train. She told him how much she liked his books but added: "Of course, I do skip some of the very dull parts once in a while; not the short dull parts but the long ones." Dickens laughed loudly and asked to be told a bit more about those long dull parts. Permission, I think, to skip.

But where to begin? Well, why not with *A Christmas Carol*? And then try *Oliver Twist* and *Nicholas Nickleby* and after that whatever takes your fancy until you come, in your own time, to *David Copperfield*, which is a better biography of the man than anyone else could write, even though the facts are made up. Make sure you get editions with pictures. That is the way his first readers read his stories, and they are part of the fun. As you read the books you may even feel that you half-recognise some of the characters and some of the descriptions in them, for in this short account I have taken words from his novels to help describe his life. In a way, it would be hard not to – for the dirty, troubled, dangerous world he described and lived in has a name: and that name is Dickensian.

And so Charles Dickens died. There is no doubt whatever about that. Yet Tiny Tim did NOT die.

Nor really did any other of his characters – not even Jacob Marley, or, at least, not his ghost who haunts us whenever we read *A Christmas Carol*. As we read their adventures, they come alive again and so does the spirit of Charles Dickens; a spirit almost as great as that of Christmas itself. Perhaps, there is no need to write:

THE END

KEY DATES

1812 Born 7th February in Portsmouth to John and Elizabeth Dickens

1822 Family moves from Chatham in Kent to London.

1824 Put to work in Warren's Blacking Factory; father imprisoned for debt.

1824-7 Resumes schooling at Wellington House Academy

1827 Finds works as a solicitor's clerk

1831 Becomes a Parliamentary reporter

1833 First story published

1834 Poor Law Amendment Act is passed

1836 *Pickwick Papers* begins publication; marries Catherine Hogarth

1837 Begins *Oliver Twist*; Mary Hogarth dies; Queen Victoria comes to the throne.

1838 Begins *Nicholas Nickleby*

1842 Travels with Catherine to the United States and Canada

1843 *A Christmas Carol* published

1848 Parliament passes act stopping women and children from working in underground mines

1849 Begins *David Copperfield*

1851 His baby daughter Dora dies; begins *Bleak House*

1853 Gives his first public reading

1856 Buys Gad's Hill Place, Rochester

1858 Separates from Catherine

1860 Begins *Great Expectations*

1867 Reading tour of America

1869 Begins writing *The Mystery of Edwin Drood*

1870 Final public readings; dies 9th June, Gad's Hill.

QUIZ

After you've finished the book, test yourself and see how well you remember what you've read.

1. Among the memorable Christmas presents that Charles Dickens received as a boy was:
   a)   An Action Man with an inflatable raft
   b)   A Noah's Ark with a set of animals
   c)   A first edition of Monopoly

2. Charles shared his father's love of:
   a)   Going for long walks
   b)   Doing jigsaw puzzles
   c)   Playing badminton

3. When Charles's father said he was suffering from 'an embarrassment of a pecuniary nature', he meant that:
   a)   He had just farted
   b)   He had money problems
   c)   He had put his shirt on inside out

4. At nine years of age, Charles would entertain people by:
   a)   Doing handstands and breakdancing
   b)   Performing impressions of King George IV
   c)   Singing songs and reciting poetry

5. Charles named the stray dog that he befriended when he was lost:
   a) Moonshine
   b) Merrychance
   c) Mudlark

6. During the 1820s, the average life expectancy in London was:
   a) 67
   b) 47
   c) 27

7. Charles left school at the age of twelve because:
   a) He joined the circus to train as a lion-tamer
   b) He went to work in a factory
   c) He got a part in a West End play

8. Charles worked twelve hours a day, six days a week. How much was he paid per week?
   a) 6 shillings
   b) 2 pounds
   c) 60 shillings

9. When John Dickens was sent to Marshalsea prison, his wife:
   a) Entered him for her favourite show, 'I'm a celebrity, get me out of jail'
   b) Sold their belongings and moved in with him
   c) Bought a caravan and took a long holiday in Scotland

10. Charles was good at his job at Warren's Blacking so the manager:
   a) Put him to work in the window as an advertisement
   b) Asked him to take charge of public relations
   c) Gave him a new suit as a reward

11. The pseudonym that Charles Dickens used for his first stories was:
   a) Viz
   b) Daz
   c) Boz

12. Charles found inspiration for the characters he wrote about by:
   a) Talking to people in chatrooms
   b) Visiting prisons and morgues
   c) Reading the lonely hearts columns

13. Charles called himself 'Mr Sparkler' because he:
   a) Had a fascination for fireworks
   b) Liked to wear women's jewellery
   c) Was full of energy and wore flashy clothes

14. When Charles, his girlfriend Nelly and her mother were involved in a train crash he:
   a) Burst into tears and begged to be rescued
   b) Coolly took charge and led them all to safety
   c) Took out a pen and paper to record the experience

15. Jacob Marley in *A Christmas Carol* is condemned to wander the world as a ghost because:
   a) He was a tight-fisted businessman
   b) He gambled away all his family's money
   c) He didn't change his underwear every day

16. Christmas trees were introduced to Britain in:
   a) The 1st century by the Romans
   b) The 11th century by the Normans
   c) The 19th century by the Victorians

17. Charles Dickens made his novels popular by:
   a) Reading them aloud at public performances
   b) Turning them into radio soap operas
   c) Giving away a free toy with every copy

18. The name of the cruel headmaster in Dickens's novel *Nicholas Nickleby* was:
   a) Wackford Squeers
   b) Ebenezer Scrooge
   c) Trotty Veck

19. When a young reader told him that she skipped the long, dull parts in his novels, Charles:
   a) Was deeply offended and stormed off
   b) Laughed and asked her to tell him more
   c) Invited her to become his editor

20. The word 'Dickensian' is used to describe:
   a) The characters and world that he wrote about
   b) The kind of clothes he liked to wear
   c) An author who writes many books

ACKNOWLEDGMENTS

ACKNOWLEDGEMENTS

It was a pleasure to read and re-read Charles Dickens for this short book. I was, however, also greatly helped by many other authors. For some of the ideas about Christmas, for example, I relied on *Dickens's Christmas: A Victorian Celebration* by Simon Callow, who besides being a fine writer and actor is our greatest living impersonator of Dickens, having even performed the role in an episode of *Doctor Who*, giving a public reading of *A Christmas Carol*. But this book would not have been written if I had not had constantly by my side Peter Ackroyd's long and magnificent biography, *Dickens*. I must thank also Alex O'Connell and Pete Hines for lending me their home in Tuscany in which to write.

Andrew Billen is a feature writer and chief TV critic on *The Times*. He previously worked for the Sheffield *Star*, *The Observer* and the London *Evening Standard* and was a television and theatre critic for the *New Statesman*. He has written two children's biographies for Short Books. He lives in Oxford with his wife and two daughters.